# POEMS FOR MOMS

## Soft Echoes of Unconditional Love

Elara F. Archer

# Index

Dear Mom,

As the pages of this book unfold, so does my heart, revealing the silent words of love and gratitude that have long danced in the quiet chambers of my soul. "Poems for Moms" is not just a collection of verses; it's a mosaic of all the moments—seen and unseen—that you, and mothers like you, have crafted with the tender artistry of your love.

To you, Mom, and to all the mothers who are reading this: you are the whispers from the heart, the soft echoes of unconditional love that resonate in our lives. This book is for you, a celebration of the laughter, the tears, the sacrifices, and the endless acts of love that define motherhood.

May these poems be a mirror, reflecting the beauty and strength you possess, and may they serve as a reminder of the irreplaceable role you play in the world. Thank you for being the first home we know, the first love we feel, and the enduring presence that guides us even when we find our wings.

With all my love,

Elara

# The First Gift

# Moment of Firsts

In the hush of dawn, our journey began,
Your heart in sync with mine, a lifelong
  plan.
For the first breath, the first cry, the first
  embrace,
I thank you, Mother, for your grace.

# Gift of Beginnings

With a tender touch, you guided my steps,
In your eyes, I saw no regrets.
A beginning so pure, a path so bright,
In your arms, the world felt right.

# The First Word: Love

Before words, our hearts conversed in love,
A language descended from the stars above.
"Mother" - the first word, a sacred sound,
In your love, my life's foundation found.

# Lessons Wrapped in Love

# Kindness Taught by Example

Your acts of kindness, a lesson so true,
Taught not by words but by the deeds you
　do.
Gratitude flows for the heart you've shown,
In your love, the best of life I've known.

# Resilience in Your Embrace

In every fall, you were my grace,
Teaching me strength in the hardest place.
For resilience, for courage, for pushing
    through,
My deepest thanks are forever due.

# The Legacy of Love

Love was the lesson in every task,
In your legacy, nothing more to ask.
For every sacrifice, every tear, every smile,
Thank you, Mother, for making it all
worthwhile.

# Echoes of Laughter, Whispers of Thanks

# Laughter in the Walls

The echoes of laughter, the joy we share,
Memories created with utmost care.
For every giggle, every chuckle, every laugh,
Thank you, Mother, for being my better
  half.

# Whispers of the Past

In quiet moments, the past whispers soft,
Of the laughter and lessons aloft.
In every whisper, a thank you is said,
For the love in which my heart was fed.

# A Symphony of Joy

Our lives, a symphony of joy and light,
With you, Mother, every note is right.
For the music, the memories, the dance of
    life,
My gratitude sings, free from strife.

# Hands That Held Mine

# Guiding Hands

Your hands, a map of tenderness and
     strength,
Guided me through life's width and length.
In every stumble, your grasp was my stand,
Thank you, Mother, for the guiding hand.

# In Gratitude for Every Lift

For every lift, after every fall,
Your hands were there, through it all.
Teaching me to rise, to face the sun,
Your support, unwavering, never undone.

# The Warmth of Your Clasp

The warmth of your clasp, a memory so
  dear,
In moments of joy, in times of fear.
For the love in your touch, the safety it
  brings,
I thank you, Mother, for the simplest of
  things.

# Wisdom's Gentle Whisper

# Silent Lessons

In the quiet moments, your wisdom speaks,
Guiding me through weeks into weeks.
With a whisper soft as dawn's first light,
You showed me what is truly right.

# The Wisdom in Your Smile

Your smile, a curve that sets things straight,
In its warmth, I find my fate.
A silent teacher of joy and resilience,
For your wisdom, I offer my reverence.

# Echoes of Your Words

Your words, like echoes in a vast hall,
Guide me back whenever I fall.
In their gentle cadence, wisdom's
    embrace,
A gratitude deep, for your grace.

# Gardens of Sacrifice and Gratitude

# Seeds of Sacrifice

In the garden of your love, sacrifices bloom,
Planted deep, in silence, they consume.
Yet from these seeds, so much beauty has
  grown,
In gratitude, the depth of your love is
  shown.

# Nurturing Growth

Your hands, weathered from care,
Tended life's garden with unwavering flair.
For every sacrifice, hidden in the night,
Thank you, Mother, for bringing dreams to
    light.

# Harvest of Heart

The harvest of your heart, a boundless field,
In its richness, your love is revealed.
For the meals missed, the sleeps forsaken,
In your love, we are awakened.

# Mirror of Her Love

# Reflections of You

In my reflection, I see more than just my
   face,
I see your strength, your grace, your
   embrace.
Traits you've woven with love's fine thread,
In your image, by your virtues, I am led.

# Inherited Light

Your light, now mine, a gift so divine,
In my actions, your character does shine.
For patience, kindness, and courage too,
Thank you, Mother, I owe much to you.

# Echoes of Her Heart

In my heart, your echoes resonate clear,
Guiding me close, drawing me near.
Your compassion, your wisdom, forever a
part,
Thank you, Mother, for the echoes of your
heart.

# Unconditional Skies, Eternal Thanks

# Beneath Your Sky

Beneath your sky, a vast expanse of blue,
Your love, a constant presence, forever
  true.
For every storm, every rain, every sun,
Thank you, Mother, for the love undone.

# The Shelter of Your Love

Your love, a shelter as wide as the skies,
Under which every hope of mine lies.
For your boundless heart, your strength,
  your care,
My eternal thanks, nothing can compare.

# Stars of Your Guidance

Like stars in the night, your guidance
    shines bright,
Leading me through, making the dark light.
For your love that guides, unwavering and
    vast,
Thank you, Mother, for the ties that last.

# Bridges Over Distance

# Love's Unseen Bridge

Across miles vast, through time and space,
Your love builds bridges, a gentle embrace.
Though apart, in my heart, you're always
  near,
Thank you, Mother, for love that draws me
  dear.

# Tethered Hearts

Separated by miles, but not at heart,
Your love, the tether, that never lets us
    part.
For every call, every letter, every shared
    dream,
Thank you, Mother, for bridging every
    stream.

# The Constancy of Your Love

Distance may define our physical state,
But your love's constancy does not abate.
Like a lighthouse guiding ships in the
  night,
Your love keeps me safe, keeps me bright.

# Legacy of Warmth: A Grateful Heart's Tribute

# Eternal Embrace

Your warmth, a cloak around my life,
Through joy, through sorrow, through
  strife.
A legacy not of gold, but of love's embrace,
Thank you, Mother, for your grace.

# The Warmth of Your Legacy

In every act of kindness, I find your
    warmth,
A legacy enduring, from south to north.
For the comfort, the peace, your love has
    sown,
Thank you, Mother, for the warmth I've
    known.

# A Heart's Tribute

To the love that shaped, that healed, that
  taught,
Your warmth, a legacy, cannot be bought.
With a heart full of gratitude, I vow to keep,
Your legacy of love, in my heart, deep.